Castle of Waves

poetry, smiles and you..!

Jugal Varu

First Printing: 2020

ISBN: 978-93-89600-30-8

Registered Address: 201A, SAS Tower, Sector 38, Gurgaon - 122003

all that this book earns
in smiles and love,
it's all for you,

Dear Maa..!

Acknowledgement

Hey You,

I am already glad if you are reading this. A book of my own, it was nowhere in my wish list until last year. In fact, I did not even use to write any of this poetry stuff. Well, I am glad that writing happened to me and now you are holding this little adventure of mine.

The list of people who helped me pursue this book goes very long. Even when the proposal for this book got rejected by few publishers, these people made sure it will be in reader's hands one day very soon – and for sure, it did happen, earlier than soon. So I would like to mention a few of these people, behind the scenes of this book.

I would first like to thank my mother, just for everything. Even though she does not get half of these poems in english language, she did read all of it and kept asking what a particular word means. She always believed in the idea of this book. Her presence and smile always made it look all of this easy and simple, and I am forever grateful for that. Love you, Mummy.

I would then thank my brother - Setu, for always boosting my faith in this book and filling the energy spot, my father for constantly asking updates about the publishing & bhabhi - Sneha for helping me add quite new words in the content.

It would have been really hard if I did not have my fun cousins in my gang. They just were there, with me, making each other laugh and that was enough. All love to Marm, Pankti, Vyom, Khushi, Neha, Samruddh, Anjana, Yatrik, Bhaumik, Pratha, Akash, Ishan, Jabali.....oops, character limit. And equally happy I am to have amazingly stupid friends for helping me dream a little big and liking these poems even WITHOUT reading it, the lazy bunch. Much love and hugs for Karan, Dhaval, Hardi, Lakhan, Vishal, Uday, Deep, Akshay, Ghata, Nidhi, Bhavin, Alex, Sohil, Harsh, Rajdeep, Kuldip, Yash, Shital, Nishi, Tanvi, Akash, Disha, Ria, Rutvi, Priyanka...I learnt a lot from all of them, but taught them back a bit more. (NOT kidding) Ok yes, kidding.

A special thanks to my father, Shweta, Harsh, Ghata and Viralee for lending their beautiful poems which you can find from Poem #99 to #103.

A very big thanks to Invincible Publishers and their entire team for making these words reach you, in form of a beautiful book and making the dream possible. I appreciate your support and co-operation through the entire stage of publishing. Thank you, again.

And a special mention for my little friend - Shaurya. I am waiting for you to grow up and read this, but hey, don't grow up!

All that this book encircles, is ultimately only for you - the readers. I thank you wholly for becoming a part of this book, in words, pages, love and many many smiles! Thank you for being the first readers. I would very much love to hear your honest reviews, better or worse. Do share your experience with me, details below.

Email : heyjugal@gmail.com
Instagram Id : HeyJugal

~ Jugal Varu

Introduction

'Castle of Waves' is a house of poetry, carved out of stories - yours and mine. This book floats on the simple idea of weaving stories of our lives into abstract poems and finding how love blooms amidst all!

A compilation of 104 poems has been marked to this book covering not only love and romance, but also a pinch of inspiration, self - love, mental wellness, etc.

'Castle of Waves' simply inculcates stories and colours of your common yet equally unique lives into poems. So any random page turned, it will be a delightful experience for the reader! And somewhere in here, you will find a bit of yourself too, wearing a silly smile!

snowfall

you hover in
the beam of my eyes,
as i hide the
stories they despise.

before i know
the colour of your smile,
you run through
the streets in dark.

we savour the taste of
each other's lips,
as the light fades
in the foggy mist.

come,
dance to this song
for times all,
till the sun melts
the night's snowfall.

and when all is
clear and bright;
call me for
another storm.

waves

when the worries of life
drench you
and shadows of dark
haunt you;

when the bright starlight
dazzles you
and realm of mirage
traps you;

when the blurred horizon
fascinates you
and trail to your home
fails you;

then, oh human!
walk to the beach
to talk with its
promising playful waves.

watch the ship sail
and the sun dissolve,
and you will return
with a scintillating smile.

and so next time,
be your own wave!

canvas

i was the canvas
white and unwithered.
then came the wolves,
sketching their desires
that can't be erased.

stories kept adding;
as a rainbow was in making
with colours
more than the seven.

and now when
the canvas turned grey,
you say i was never an art.
but i know,
even grey galaxies
make a perfect art.

flutter

that night
the air felt blue and pink.

the way your eyes danced
to find me in the lot,
and how they gleamed
at the sight of me.

i knew,
this time,
you were about to stay.
and this made
my heart flutter
with fear of love.

smell

of water lilies
and fresh mint leaves,
your breath is still
my favourite smell.

barter

i have bartered
enough love for poems
and too many words
for promises.

and so,
when you ask me this,
for sure,
i will barter
all my smiles;
to witness
a few of yours.

sweet

out of stars,
poetry and colours,
what will
you smile at?

don't ask me back.
for all the sweet nothings
you whispered in my heart,
gave me all of those;

and so right now,
i am smiling at you.

whisper

how do I look,
you ask
grinning in your
black dress.

and i lean closer
to whisper
in your ears,
"exactly...mine."

oblivion

the sparkle
in your eyes
was my horizon.

the flair
of my skin
was your boat;

our
entwined fingers
were the paddles.

and somewhere,
our bodies
dived into oblivion.

poetry

hey you,
tonight,
play with my hair,
pour out your fears
and
smile with your eyes;

and i tell you,
by the next night,
you will be my poetry.

enough

you are enough art,
for a human.
with conversations
long like winter nights
and mystery in your eyes
as if hidden at horizon.

you are enough art,
with silence
melted in our breaths
and hearts beating
like a light year.

you are enough art,
even with all the grey;
'cause you are a galaxy,
even without stars.

stranger

waiting in the lounge
you look into my eyes,
and ask if I ever
share stories with
strangers?

and i deny;
but somehow, we pass the night.
because when dawn breaks,
you seem no stranger
to my heart.

ruffle

she missed him
spoiling and ruffling
her hair;

while he missed
swooning over the sight,
as she set her
fluttering hair
back in the place.

carved

it is not easy
to love me,
with my flawed solitude.

but you carved
a way out,
down to my soul;
and i knew
i wasn't a secret,
anymore.
love finally found me.

scars

his words
were scribbling.
and reading this,
her scars were healing.

on yellow old pages,
the ink dried;
and somewhere,
the tears.

lost

you and me
seem to be lost
in the blotted corners
of this house;

let's find us,
making it our
home again.

laughter

on some nights,
i secretly wish
you sing me a song.

but then,
you crack a stupid joke
and laugh on your own.
and i realize;
your laughter is
my favourite song!

Henn Kim

lamp-post

when your
starlit face
gets a bit
hazy,

can i be
your tiny
sunbeam?

just like the
lamp-post
at the end
of tunnel.

lyrics

in quest of finding
that perfect tune;

did you realize,
the lyrics of
your life changed
somewhere?

moonlit

in moonlit corridors,
to the gentle tunes
of wind chime,
we dance.

we dance and talk,
till our hearts carry
no weight.

then we lay
on the swing in silence
except for the random creaks.

i wake up to the sound of
birds chirping
and you snoring.
i look at you
and hide your face
from sunlight.

and i come to know;
you are the one
i want to dance
all my dances with.

breeze

she asked me,
if i ever
care to share.

but let me ask her,
will she dare to care?
will she stay?
or fall out like
the autumn leaves?

but we talked
and the coffee mugs
kept refilling,
and i knew,
she will be my poetry,
for every night.

home

hey love,
let's build our home.

with friendship as its pillars
and walls built of memories.
coated with togetherness,
painted blue with textures
of silly giggles
and happy smiles.

furnished with glitters
of hugs and kisses;
little but ours,
isn't it amazing?

for it is,
low on budget,
high on love.

playful

times later,
if ever
someone will close my eyes
from behind,
i won't know who
it will be;
but i know one thing.
it will never be you,
with your long playful fingers.

sail

and when you are ready,
we will sail between
colour, smiles and waves.

till then,
i will paint
every grey shade
of your life;
with every colour
i can find.

black

on hazy mornings
and blue nights,
i dress up in
your favourite black.
telling you about
my busy day at work,
but you never
talk about yours.

and so,
even I won't tell you.
how my heart aches every night,
how empty my fingers feel
and how I wake up next morning,
again in black;
only to talk to your grave.

chase

rushing to destinations
and leaping through
the roads,
take a small walk back
before huddling
for your next race.

collect the smiles dropped by
and tears soaked in roads,
else they all lose your trace.

for you will need them,
once your chase ends
and you see,
just the dark wall.

ashes

i was building
a sandcastle,
waiting for it to drown
by these playful waves
carrying your ashes;

you are still there, right?

flowers

embrace even the thorns,
ultimately
they will lead you
to flowers and hearts.

pearls

beauty is in the
starlit sky,
just like in the mess of
dusty clouds.

beauty is in the
dazzling sunlight,
just like in
the pearls of fog.

but you know,
what is always beautiful?
you.
even in a mess
or with a tiara.
you will shine.

autumn

the blue curtains
still hang,
at the window
still broken.

the autumn leaves twirl
as the wind swipes through.
go walk through them,
before it's a long summer.

but hey,
just like the broken blues
will your heart stay the same?
because i will be autumn
for all your days.

cluster

just for a while,
look up.

the clusters of stars
are dimming,
rays of sun are
smiling for hope,
the colours of
rainbow need the
perfect shade of your smile.

but just keep your
heart locked;
for i am selfish,
to not share you
with any.

for once

for once,
come home tonight.

your daughter wants
you to tuck her in bed,
for once.

that photo frame
is still empty,
waiting for you to
select a picture of us,
for once.

i found video
of our prom night.
do you ever recall
that night?

and even if you
wish to just drink,
i will too,
for once.
i bought wine glasses
today, two.
but for once,
come home.

void

let go off the fist,
water will drop out
anyway.
leaving traces of void,
just like people.

but for once,
open your heart.
and you will know;
the skies are waiting to rain.

bubble

you gaze at the starlit sky,
i look into your story-teller eyes.

you run for the distant horizon,
i walk to the shore in you.

you play with the
chaos and storm,
i bubble my
safety home in you.

you rip off the thoughts
of my dark nights,
and here i am,
planting love to live you,
a bit more.

umbrella

the sky looks clear,
the wind blows blue,
but hey you,
tell me;

"can we still walk
under one umbrella
together?"

wars

writing words, to build an art
is not my way,
and i get it.
for too many sad puns
don't make a good poem.

but you waged wars
with words and love;
and yet, lost it all.
tell me at least,
can i be your muse now?

horizon

i look at you
and wonder if
this is what
lies at the
scintillating
corners of
horizon;

a mystery unexplored,
yet poetic.

glass

this time,
if the glass breaks,
don't collect its pieces.

the weight in your bag
is too heavy,
for once, drop it off.

your heart is just the same,
let it float.

and now when
you find a new glass;
don't hold it unless
it reflects your heart
with joy and light.

faces

drizzling rain outside
and coffee steaming in your cup,
you look around,
for faces with stories.

the man with newspaper
seemed too boring
and the couple to your left,
too lost in love.

a woman kept yelling
and her husband
kept drinking.
the other guy,
staring and
sketching you.

nothing interests you
but the moist on window.

so you take a photo
from your wallet,
and write a story
for the same face;
again like always,
ever since it left.

footprints

for one last time,
come,
let's walk
to the beach
and leave
no footprints.

just like i failed
to leave mine,
on the traces
of your heart.

spot

you deny my love,
saying white spots on your skin
are not to be loved,
you are not to be loved.

but i fear,
my life will be a
bigger spot, void,
if without you;

and so you let my words
fill the spot
between our lips.

her world

her world was little.
her happiness too,
safely tucked in
my childhood pictures
and keys of her broken typewriter.
her worries stuffed in a jar
as she rushes
at the 4th whistle of pressure cooker
to make that perfect dal
and carefully adding exactly
two spoons of sugar,
just the way
my father wanted his tea.

winters passed and father left home,
making her world even more little.
but she still makes his tea
and every night,
her smile fades into nothing.
she writes me letters
and i finally come home
with a new typewriter.
a year later,
a book with her name
rests on my shelf.

and at last i watch;
her world was getting bigger,
'cause now even she was a part
in her world.

little

your letters have
turned yellow,
but those words
still smile.

your front teeth
are missing,
but your wide grin
still lives.

and all these winters later,
a little you, a little me
and a lot of us
is
still my home.

again

let's have a pillow fight, again.
endless coffee talks at balcony, again.
selfies in one t-shirt, again.
spend on love, again.
become us, again.

empty

i am here
after all this while,
where a while means
eight long winters.

wondering how
we would have danced
all our summer nights;
had you stayed then.

but morning peeps in like
a silent song
where i find
your side of bed,
still empty.
till then,
i will write
for next summers and winters.

stolen

there lies a smile.

in stolen glances
and secret kisses in narrow streets.

in kindness of a stranger
and smell of water lilies.

in travels to new cities
and their amber lights.

in walking at the beach
and writing your name on sand.

in watching old photo albums
and missing a friend or two.

and maybe,
there lies a smile,
even in reading this.

closure

you and me
are just the same.
creatures of night
waiting for the night to fall
and stars to dance.
because sleep somehow
does not share its part
with our gleaming eyes.

for we have too many sad stories
of the same person,
yours always incomplete
and mine always untouched.
cos we never asked
and they never told.

so tonight,
lets share those words
over wine or coffee.
and we might bring closure
to that story after all;
well at least,
for either one of us.

blend

like the colours
that don't blend,
words that don't
fit in a poem,
stars that don't
form a constellation,
you and me,
are just the same.

but our eyes talked
stories of our hearts;
and i knew
we would build a home,
to fix our broken wings
and rest our incomplete stories.

stories

your eyes have stupid stories to tell,
but i don't mind listening to them
until your jaws get tired,
eyes shut to rest;
and the locks of your hair
dance to the music
of your tiny snores!

rains

i have questions to ask.

when you see him
smile in daylight,
do you think of
glittery stars?

when he runs to
the beach waves,
do you notice the
trail of his
footprints?

when he hops wildly
in the rains,
do you join him
to dance?

and now when you sleep
on terrace without
his arms as your pillow,
do the same stars
scare you?

train

a train
speeding through cities
and you
tripping through hearts.
if ever,
words get heavier
and silence becomes unbreathable,
just know;
the train is still running
and your home is yet to come,
don't settle for any less.

city

on some nights,
as i switch
sides to sleep,
you come for a while,
storming in my dreams,
draining me of sleep
and flooding with
memories.

they let me out
on a stroll;
to the roads we walked,
corners where we kissed
and smiles that we lived,
all over the city.

the night has passed;
and then i return
to the point where you left,
alone in the lights.

but it is okay,
for you will visit me
at night again,
maybe.
or i can try to
sleep tonight,
maybe.

shore

on a certain night,
walking down the
crowded street,
you will find a heart,
as lonely as yours;

which will keep
coming back.
just like the
waves keep coming
to kiss the shore.

yellow

the pages have grown
yellow and battered
and the words too heavy,
yet you never burn them.

for you know,
the ashes of his letters
would be heavier
than your heart.

you read a note,
at the fireplace;
"i have sent you letters,
read them tonight."

and so you do,
every night
battering the same letter,
more and more.

locked

may be
its no one's fault.

for my eyes
talked too much
and you read them
straight to the core.

this feared my heart;
now, what will be
our story like?

will it be
locked in my eyes too?
or set free;
like the waves
in the sea.

streets

grey and wrinkled,
the old man lived it all.

a beloved he lost,
with her youth and colours.
so streets he roamed
in search of her breath.

and then everyday,
when dried his tears;
balloons he sold
and smiles he bought.
and this is how,
the old man
could live it all.

rings

breathe my air
and you will blow
rings of smoke
beautiful than
your cigar puffs.

traverse my skin
and you will walk
roads darker than
the cold nights.

hold my hand
and you will get
my smiles brighter than
the sunshine.

and when its night,
i will write you words
that will stay
longer than our promises.

rooftop

for tonight,
just stay,
after we make love.
before you start to leave,
come
lie on the rooftop.

now tell me,
what do you love more,
the moon or the stars?

but don't ask me;
for you are my
whole damn sky.

arms

I just know.
your arms will be my pillow
for all my nights,
even as you
slid your hand back gently;
after I blow tiny snores,
in all your nights.

the other side

you know
its all right.

to still wear his shirt
and sleep,
to walk on the street
you first met,
to give a happy closure
to his incomplete poetry,
to look at the stars
just like you smiled
at his eyes;

because somewhere
he is smiling too,
across the other side.

concert

walk with me
in the starry nights
and foggy mornings.

run with me bare foot
at the shore as we
catch the waves.

laugh with me as i dress
in your clothes
and sing you live concerts.

hide beneath the blankets
with me as the music rises
in that horror movie.

play with me and sometimes,
allow me to cheat.
you love me, right?

ride your bike with me
on streets of that village
with church and forts.

just keep talking
through eyes,
and you will
never lose us.

neon

i would trade
all the stars
in the sky,
for all those
stolen glances
in hallways
and secret long kisses
under backstreet neon lights.

because with you,
i am getting
the whole galaxy.

scattered

scattered,
raw and unfiltered,
is what i am.

so if you intend to stay,
come
sit with me
under the stars
and we will make
poetries.

and maybe some morning,
my heart won't be scattered,
anymore.

want

i know.
you never wanted
the stars,
but to just gaze
at the starlit sky.

you never wanted
fireflies trapped
in your jar,
but to enjoy the sight,
as they fly.

you never wanted
pretty filters,
but only the core beauty,
raw and scarred.

you never believed
in miracles,
but somehow,
you became one.

and then one day,
you held his hand
and filled the void.
and that i know,
you will always want.

tides

for now,
the days are sour
and nights are long.

but know this.
when tides will be high,
i will keep coming to you,
in parts,
back and forth.
until the waves keep
kissing the shore.

jigsaw

with a zillion pieces
scattered around,
my jigsaw puzzle
is nowhere to be fixed.

but then, you breathe closer
and say it doesn't matter,
'cause with you
there will be a new jigsaw
with only one piece;
the whole of me.

flames

you crave a different warmth,
the one from the flames
glowing red and orange,
burning words of letters
and smiles of pictures.

but your heart chokes
from the black of its smoke.
and so,
take out what's left
of those flames.

and maybe,
your heart can trace again;
those pink blushes
and blue promises.

sugar

when its all over,
reach out for the
pieces that lay shatter.
and lock it in
your jar.

but just don't pluck
out the happy ones;
because too much of sugar
will leave a black trail
for your heart.

and you already have
had enough of that.

pebbles

cities apart,
you revel in
amber lights and stranger faces
every night.

i am still here,
under the same tree,
by the river you threw
pebbles at.

now that the river has dried,
i am collecting those pebbles
and that tree is a mere skeleton
without its leaves;

i wonder,
is my photo
still in your wallet?
or did you find a new face
to calm your night?

wrinkles

sitting in the verandah,
your hair grey
and skin wrinkled.
and in those
subtle moments,
you see your life,
flashing back whole.

in the pool of faces
that come across,
i want to know.
did you find me
in the crowd?

and if yes,
i want,
for one last time,
the kiss of your wrinkles.

breathe

you sit
in dim lights,
reeking with cheap alcohol
and floor covered in
cigar butts.
how hardly you could breathe?

yet daily, she steps in this mess
and gets you water lilies
clearing the night.
you have to ask,
why does she care?

and she tells you,
she wants a home in here.
in you, with you.
and so this night;
you could breathe.

red

stop at the traffic signal.
on red light, you see
cars washed and pennies thrown.
headlines shouted and windows closed.
mirrors adjusted and smiles exchanged.
a scratch made and collars caught.
balloons flying and bread crumpled.

the green light hits;
and you drive off
for the same stories
at another red.

frame

i have tried all.

flowers that fail
to cover your scent.

new cushions
keeping me awake,
unlike your arms.

fairy lights and amber lamps,
dimmed by your
moonlit face in a frame.

all these,
'cause you never return.
what am I to do now?
burn this home
or bring more flowers at day;
and wait for another night.

art

its an art.

to walk with the waves
barefoot on a beach.
to sleep under the stars
on a full moon.
to help an old lady
cross the road.
to once not blame your mother
for less salt in food.
to play with marbles with kids
in summer holidays.
to not always take a
new road alone.

its an art;
to be carefree,
to be happy,
to be you.

and just sometimes,
its an art
to make you think on this.

wildfire

building homes
in stranger hearts
and leaving sparks
like wildfire,
you keep adding
scars to your stories.

why not settle
for a nearby home?
a less curious
and more known.

and then maybe,
you will see the waves
that cease the fire
and wipe your scars.

traces

tonight.
kiss me hard
until air feels lost.
let your beads of sweat
run over my skin.
clench my thighs
with all your might.
scar my back
in any random art.

but next morning,
please leave.
without keeping
any colour of love
and trace of my smile.

hues

in hues of sunlit mornings
and blues of cold nights,
we took breaths
in giggles and tears.
this habit we weaved
and named it home.

we aged together
through autumns and storms,
sipping wines and
talking of stars
in our own sky.

and now, so many autumns later,
i look for you
among the stars
in this cold night,
drinking your favourite wine
wishing you were still mine;
and not far in that sky.

wrecked

your ship wrecked me
deep in the ocean
in the name of love,
when my wings fluttered to fly.

but now I know;
i need to be
my own sailor.

shivering

i will always remember.

the glint in your eyes
after your swim.
and also your
body shivering with cold.

your laugh when i
tripped from the bench.
and your tears when you
talked of your father.

the letters you wrote
and yellow roses
tucked in it.

the walk at the beach
and stories we talked
under the stars.

how much you loved
the colour black
and hated red.

but do you remember
the colour of my smile?
or the last time
i wrote you a poem?
you don't.
and so, i am still writing it.

whisper

even after years apart,
in the midst of a night,
all i want to hear is
words, you whispered that night,
our last night.

too easy to recall,
too hard to grasp;
"i will see you tonight."

clown

to all the strangers who smiled
and to the little gang in their bicycles.

to all the granny gossiping in courtyard
and to all the old men laughing in the park.

to all the backbencher artists at school
and to all the pink blush brewing there.

to all the waves in the sea
and to all the sparrows bickering
unanimously in that tree;

word on the street is,
you all share smiles for free.
and so today,
this clown needs one.

relief

you once told,
love is the relief
when your scars
start to heal.
and i believed you.

but i hear somewhere,
it is also the
carnage and open wounds
left to scar.
and now, i believe it too.
because today,
you are my scar.

unfiltered

when the night falls
stay up till late
with a few stars,
a gloomy moon
and unfiltered me;

and together,
we will show you colours
more than the seven
of your sunny rainbows.

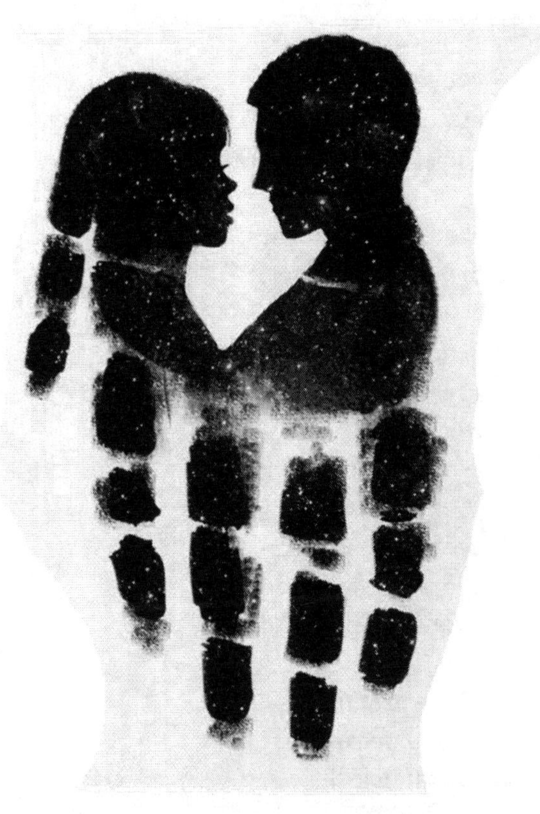

ashes

you left,
but parts of you
still give me company.

like the broken keys
of your typewriter,
dried blue roses
in my books,
your angry face
when i beat you
in arm wrestling,
your joyous eyes
every time you see a kid
and the laughs you had
after your pranks on me.

all these still here;
maybe because
our sandclock
runs on your ashes.

walk out slow

if it weren't for the nights,
i would have nothing
to come home to.

except
for the fan,
humming from the ceiling
in sync with the tape,
that plays my mother's songs.
your smell still resting,
on the crumpled bed sheet
where you smiled at my closed eyes.
and blurred by the smoke I blow
after our long goodbye kiss at the doorstep,
i watch you walk out slow.

and these words i write
in this dark night,
will always be my home;
to come.

galaxy

when our lips will
end the distance,
a star will
join another.

so now,
when you look
at the galaxy;
will you find that star?

and if not,
we can add one more star.
‘cause for me,
you are already
my galaxy of stars.

promises

i don't want
to believe in
the stories of promises.

all i want is,
now.
and mornings with you
where shadows of your smile
are cast upon me,
warm and bright.

cigarettes

watch me through the day,
tripping and smiling.
then counting the stairs to my office
and puffing that many cigarettes.

on my way back in the bus,
watch me play with the kid beside.
and then kicking a creep in his groin
to make him 'feel'.

now when its dark,
walk me to the beach and leave,
but don't watch me;
for i will be writing
about you then, smiling.

stay

nights, i wish were longer
to complete my poems
and this bottle of wine
filled with your songs.

for i have had enough voices
that sing the same song
where all are gone
by the first ray of sun.

for once,
i want to finish this poem
and gulp the wine in full;
and so i wish,
for nights to be long
and you to stay,
for one more song.

believed

i never believed.
a heart
cold as ice
and eyes
blue as night
could ever melt in
warmth of haze
and shut to rest
without nightmares.

but then,
you told me
even the sun
embraces the moon
once in a while.

and I knew;
you were my eclipse
for every rise and fall.

home

home.
that no longer
feels like.

except the furry doormat
once i slipped on,
the sunbeam peeping
through the broken window.
and dead plants
that i no longer water.

but there is no you
to dance with me
at terrace in rainy nights.

i can't smell you anymore.
and so i am burning
all flowers in your garden.

names

walk by the beach,
for the sea
breathes infinite stories.

every name scrawled
on the beach and
every sandcastle built
by little hands,
the waves swallow it all.

yet the waves keep coming back;
why do they?
for more stories
or to puke back some;
'cause some stories end in tears,
even the seas can't
carry enough salt.

pieces

tear all our pictures,
i will collect all hundred pieces.
burn all those yellow roses,
i will still water its ashes.
rush to your distant lands,
i will write our names on sand
every time, the waves wash it off.

and on some nights,
if you look at the sky and smile,
i will smile too;
because at least
you can't break this sky,
like you did
to mine - you.

faint

how much you loved,
a random stranger
smiling at you.

and now,
how much you dread
the faint smile
of my love;
when we became
known strangers.

witness

it is simple.
i want to witness
your cheeks hurt
with laughter
and skin getting
wrinkled,
as we walk
on this same road;
for nights and years.

mirage

on summer beach sands,
with a tear
forcing out of my eye,
i ask you to stare
at the horizon.

but you look
at me instead
and tell me;
you have caught
the mirage,
that my eyes confide.
and so i can let,
the waves flow.

rose

stand by me amidst
all the thorns;
and together
we will find
our perfect rose!

વાતો

વીતી જાય
આ વરસાદની ઉંમર,
તે પહેલા ચાલ ને
કરીએ થોડી વાતો;

એક ખોબો ભરાઈ એટલી તારી
ને આ ટીપાં ઝીલવાઈ એટલી મારી.

છેવટે તો છે તારી આંખો ની બધી આ વાત,
એમાં મારા શબ્દો ની શું વિસાત..!

એવું પણ બને

એવું પણ બને,
અંતર ના પડઘાઓ શબ્દો માં સંભળાય જાય ને
હૃદયની લાગણીઓ આંખમાં વંચાઈ જાય.

એવું પણ બને,
તારી આંખોમાં જોઈને દિલમાં સમાઈ જવાય ને
વરસતા વરસાદમાં ક્યારેક આંખો પણ ભીંજાય જાય.

એવું પણ બને,
મારા અવાજ માં પણ તારો સાદ સંભળાય જાય ને
વળગીને છાતીએ રહેવા વાળા હાથમાં થી છૂટી જાય.

એવું પણ બને,
ખુશીઓ ભરેલી મુઠ્ઠી માંથી
ખબર ના રહે અને હાથ માંથી સરી જાય ને
સુવડાવીને કોઈ ને ભરઊંઘમાં
તારા ગણવા પડે આખી રાતમાં.

એવું પણ બને,
હસાવતા કોઈની
પાંપણ ભીંજાય જાય ને
ફરીયાદ કરતા કોઈની
યાદ ઝબૂકી જાય.

- Deepak Varu

તહેવાર

એક અલ્લડ છોકરી ને એનો બાળપણનો પ્રેમ.
પહેલી એ પ્રીત વળી ભૂલવી પણ કેમ?
આમ તો હવે ખાસ જો કે થાય ના કંઈ વાત.
ને થાય તો પણ એમાં છે શી મોટી વાત?
આમ તો એ વાર્તા હવે જૂની થઈ ગઈ,
અમ પ્રીત કેરી શેરી એ સુની થઈ ગઈ.
કેવા એકમેક પર અમે વરસ્યા કરતા!
ને એક ક્ષણ પામવાને તરસ્યા કરતા!

જો કે,
કેમ છો? કેમ નહીં? નો વ્યવહાર હજી રાખ્યો છે,
રોજ નહિ, પણ ગમવાનો તહેવાર હજી રાખ્યો છે.
ને એવો આવ્યો અવસર જેને તરસ્યા કરતા,
પણ હવે એ ક્યાં ખોવાયા, જે વરસ્યા કરતા?

શબ્દો તો સમજું, મૂઆ બોલે ન કંઇ,
આખ્યું થી બે ઘડી કૈંક વાતું તો થઈ.
આંખોમાં વણકહ્યું શૈશવનું હેત,
શબ્દો સમજણાં એ કેમ કરી કે'ત ?

- Shweta 'Hemadri' Pandya

a wish

beneath a constellation,
with a contemplating face,
wished a fall of a star;
for a wish to make.

closed my eyes swiftly
and made the wish quickly;
the clandestine wish,
was her happiness.

- Harsh Trivedi

introvert

it was love at first words
when the introvert girl answered
to his question asking her birth date.
to a great wonder, even he shared the
same birth date - 18th November.

eyes talked, stories began
and finally 3 cakes were lit together,
2 birth day cakes and one
for their wedding day.

- Ghata Vasani

मुस्कुराहट

बारिश की एक एक बूंद
जब धरती पर गिरती है
और मिटटी अपनी खुश्बू फैलाती है
तब तेरी याद आ जाती है।
सूरज की जब पहली किरण
मेरी चेन से सोयी बंद आखो पे पड़ती है
तब तेरी याद आ जाती है।

सांज ढलने पर पंछी
अपने बसेरे पर लोटता है
बच्चो के लिए दाना लेकर,
तब तेरी याद आ जाती है।
चाँद अपनी चांदनी बिखेर कर
सुबह खुद तो चला जाता है
पर जो एक सुकून छोड़ जाता है
उस वक्त तेरी याद आ जाती है।

बस हर वक्त तेरी याद ही आती है
तू कभी नही आता ;
में तो भूल ही गयी थी
जो दिल के करीब होते है
उनकी शिकायते नहीं की जाती
सिर्फ याद किया जाता हे।
इसीलिए,
हर वक्त तेरी याद आ जाती है
और मुस्कुराहट वापस आ जाती हे।

- Viralee Keraliya

castle of waves

for one last night,
come.
let's dance
for the stars
and converse with eyes.

i know
you will spend
your moonlit smile
as i read you my poems.

and in all these moments,
i will capture the sight
of my
castle of waves,
which was all this time;
all of you.

- Jugal Varu

Thank You!